From the Kitchen Table…Thoughts

From the Kitchen Table...Thoughts

Lynne Voutsinas M.D.

Writers Club Press
San Jose New York Lincoln Shanghai

From the Kitchen Table...Thoughts

All Rights Reserved © 2000 by lynne voutsinas m.d.

No part of this book may be reproduced or transmitted in any form or by any means, graphic, electronic, or mechanical, including photocopying, recording, taping, or by any information storage retrieval system, without the permission in writing from the publisher.

Writers Club Press
an imprint of iUniverse.com, Inc.

For information address:
iUniverse.com, Inc.
620 North 48th Street, Suite 201
Lincoln, NE 68504-3467
www.iuniverse.com

ISBN: 0-595-13758-X

Printed in the United States of America

Dedicated to my husband Danny,
who helps me be the best I can be

To my son Nicholas, who taught me
everything I know

To my daughter Alexandra, for completing my dream

Acknowledgements

Thanks to Nicholas Voutsinas for his Editorial assistance.

Contents

Acknowledgements vii

Love and Marriage 1
Children and Parents 17
Money 63
Religion 73
Health 85
People 93

Love and Marriage

When looking for a husband, decide which ten things are most important to you.

If you get one, two and seven you are doing very well. However, it is very hard to live without three, four, five, and six.

When to marry...

When you meet someone without whom you would not be the best you can be.

People should marry three times.

First for sex.

Second for children.

Third for companionship.

How fortunate are those who need marry only once.

Men get married when they are settled in their careers.

Women get married when they are asked.

I think that two people can learn to love each other if they are both

willing, open and honest.

Marriage takes place in the bedroom. That doesn't only mean sex. Marriage is between two people when they are alone together. When no one else is there.

Some marriages are inclusive, others exclusive, even to their children.

My husband always says " Men win a few battles, but women win the war"

People who are married do not necessarily have better marriages than people who are divorced. They just prefer to be married and hopefully to each other.

Remember, if you can't get along with a person when you are married, it must be impossible once you are divorced.

We all know weddings are for the bride. When planning a wedding consider that you are not spending all that money for a five hour party, but rather a year of planning it all.

My husband and I probably won't get divorced because he dislikes change more than I do.

Once you have children, you are in each other's lives forever.

Divorce not only affects your children, but also your grandchildren.

CHILDREN AND PARENTS

It's one thing if you choose not to have children. It's another if you can't.

There are some women who were meant to have a lot of children. I just wasn't one of them.

The worst thing you can say to a woman who is having difficulty either conceiving or carrying a baby to term is: "At least you can enjoy trying."

Some women enjoy being in a group. Others prefer one-on-one relationships. The women who enjoy being in a group probably enjoy having many children and are good at managing them.

I knew I was pregnant with a boy because he took over my body.

I knew I was pregnant with a girl because she took over my mind.

The definition of natural childbirth: You carried the baby for nine months and the baby came out of your body, whether by Caesarian or vaginal delivery, with pain medication or without.

The hardest thing I had to do was leave my son when I was in labor with my daughter.

How the first child feels about your love when the second one comes along.

If I say I love you with all my heart and all my love I give to you then if I had any more love I would give it to you.

Therefore, I must have to take some away from you to give to the new baby because if I had anymore love I would give it to you.

> Simple arithmetic

Remember children really believe in Santa Claus and The Tooth Fairy. They don't think in the abstract. They deal in concrete thought and fantasy.

I spend too much time documenting my life and that of my children instead of actually enjoying the moment.

The fear of something happening to your child is overwhelming. It is only surpassed by the fear that one of your children might irreparably harm the other.

Raising children is joy. There is an element of sadness as they grow up. You sort of miss the baby, the toddler and the child at different ages, even as you enjoy each moment and stage of development remarking how great one is and how wonderful three is. They grow up right before your eyes. Sometimes you can't recall the baby or toddler they were.

The most important things you can teach your children is to love themselves, to not be jealous and never do anything to harm themselves.

The first child gets 100%.
The second child gets 50%.
The third child gets 25%.

The second child comes from a used uterus.

If you watch babies, it seems as if they are trying to talk, but their muscles aren't strong enough to actually say words. This is no different from their back and leg muscles not being strong enough to allow them to walk.

When my son was a toddler, I would say, "I don't like my daughter-in-law and she's not even born yet."

I think my son is easy because I perceive him to be like me and therefore I know how he wants to be comforted. He used to think I could read his mind.

It is very difficult when your child has a talent that you don't have and therefore are unable to help them. It is frustrating for them and you feel inadequate.

I always answer my child's questions. If it is a topic I'm not comfortable answering, I try and think of my response before he asks. I often look for a children's book on the subject. I believe if I don't give him an answer then when it is an important issue he won't feel comfortable asking me.

Mothers give comfort.

Fathers give confidence.

Women have children.

Men have families.

Why is it when you walk into a woman's office you see pictures of her children, while men have pictures of their wives and children? If he doesn't have his wife's picture something may be amiss.

My husband stays home with our children. This alleviates my anxiety when I go to work. It doesn't stop my desire of wanting to be there. I still want to go to the school play, class trip and be class mom.

Men can be warm, loving and nurturing. They can be wonderful fathers but they cannot replace the mother. Children need their mother.

When do you stop needing your mother?

Men and women think differently about children. For men, the children ate a bag of chips, at least they ate. For women it has to be a balanced meal.

For men, the children were in a chlorinated pool all day, so they don't need a bath. For women, the children were in a chlorinated pool all day, which is why they need a bath.

Mothers of sons cannot be feminists. It's mutually exclusive.

A son for a woman is an opportunity to live vicariously. A chance to watch him do all the things you can't or couldn't do because you are a woman. You also don't know in advance the things he will have to endure growing up as you would a daughter.

A son for a man is an opportunity to have an intimate relationship with another man and have it be OK.

A daughter for a man is life's revenge. All the things they did to women they now fear will be done to their daughters.

Remember you had your last good night's sleep the day before you became pregnant.

It is difficult to get up with an infant, but at least you know where they are and that they are safe. It must be incredibly difficult to give your child the keys to the car for the first time.

Always make your children feel as if it is their home. Then, hopefully, they will want to bring their friends around when they are teenagers. That is when you really want to see what is going on.

It may be important to be home when your children are infants or toddlers, but it is even more important to be home when they are adolescents.

If you don't listen to your children at three and four then at thirteen and fourteen they won't talk to you when it may really matter.

Babies cannot be spoiled. They cannot manipulate. They don't think like adults with all their experience and knowledge. They cry for a reason. It is part of how they communicate to get their needs met.

Mothers who stay home don't necessarily spend any more time with their children than mothers who work outside the home. They just have more opportunity to do so.

Quality time is bogus. You need a minimal quantity to make it quality.

Babies know when you are with them and paying attention to them and when you are with them and not paying attention to them.

The most precious thing you can give someone is your time, because you can never get it back.

Why do they teach children in kindergarten that they should be friends with everyone when that is not possible or realistic? Why not teach them that you do not have to be friends or even like one another but you have to get along? You may have to sit at the same table or even do a project together. That's real life.

It angers me to know that women in prison (who may have committed crimes) can keep their children with them until they are a year of age while I had to go to work six weeks after the birth of my son because I am a doctor.

Playground politics....

Interacting with the parents of your children's friends and classmates. It can often be difficult, sometimes even treacherous.

What do you say when your child no longer wants to be friends with a classmate and you and the mother have become good friends?

What do you tell your child when they haven't been invited to a party? Do you say anything to the parents?

What do you tell a longtime friend when your child doesn't like his or her child?

These are all lessons in life for both you and your child. Remember to choose your battles wisely. Teach the same to your child.

Money

Looking for a house is like looking for a husband. You always settle.

You cannot invest in everything.

Don't be sorry about not having invested more money in something that did well. It's all a gamble.

If all your investments are doing well at the same time, you are doing something wrong.

No one can tell you what risk you are willing to take financially.

Money gives you choices.
Choices give you freedom.

It may be wise to buy the least expensive house in the most expensive neighborhood you can afford. However, services (lawn care, plumbing, electrical work, painting etc.) will reflect the neighborhood, not the actual cost.

Cheap is not about money.

You can be cheap with your time and emotions.

Cheap is a state of mind.

Religion

Heaven and Hell are right here on earth. Could anything be worse than losing a child? Could anything be better than a baby born healthy?

Hope is an amazing thing. Against all odds you can still have hope, especially when a loved one has been diagnosed with a terminal illness. Even as they are dying you can have hope. If you take away their hope they die. Perhaps the will to live is just that-HOPE.

A young man was watching as his father was dying. He asked me if this was living. I wanted to say yes. This is dying and dying is a stage of life.

There is no such thing as etiquette in grief. How did he take it? Did he take it well? What does that mean? He took it. He had no choice. He took it anyway he could.

It is very interesting that many religions have similar mourning rituals, just the sequence may be different, but the time frame of grieving is the same.

People who intermarry want to intermarry.

Intermarriage may be the solution to prejudice.

I don't understand how you can raise a child of intermarriage in a single culture. It denies their other parent. It denies half of who they are.

Intermarriage must be healthy. Mutts are healthier than purebreds and the risk of inherited genetic disorders is markedly diminished.

If your child intermarries, you always have someone for your own religious holidays. You need not share with their in-laws.

Health

I believe the brain is like a muscle that must be exercised or it atrophies.

Most thin people do not eat a lot. They don't think about food. It may seem that they eat a lot but they may not even eat everyday.

You can either be thin or eat cake.

If your biological clock is preset then I think people who get diseases in their youth that are commonly seen in the elderly probably have a shorter life span. Usually the disease will be a more virulent form. People who get diseases later in life that are found in childhood may have a longer life span.

Why don't we study the people who don't get the disease? For instance, the person who smokes and doesn't get cancer or heart disease? Why does one person who smokes get heart disease and not lung cancer? For some people it takes only one cigarette, for others a lifetime of smoking. Each person must have an Achilles heel, an organ system that is predisposed to illness, given the right circumstance.

People

The saddest thing in the hospital is a patient without visitors.

Some people have no filter between their brain and their mouth.

Why do people find it necessary to exaggerate how long their infant sleeps at night and markedly underestimate how long their commute really is?

We all don't want the same things in life. That is why there are over one hundred different kinds of cars and we are all not married to the same man.

People who choose to be writers, actors, singers or other professions in the arts have to want it more than life itself because of the uncertainty.

People who are very successful in their careers, be it sports, business medicine, or acting, must be brilliant in their own way. If they weren't, they would have not reached the top.

I used to think that there were three kinds of people:

Those that know,

Those that think they know

and those that have no idea.

Now I know that we all have no idea.

Some people are born risk takers others are physically cautious.

People don't change they just acquire more responsibility and appear to change.

People go into medicine for four reasons: money, power, prestige and to help people. Some only for money, some only for power, some only for prestige and some only to help people. But, for most it is a combination.

If someone says they don't study, they are either lying or doing poorly.

Everyone must study no matter how intelligent they are. It is a matter of concentration. What takes one person an hour may take another three hours. The first person can sit down, focus and remember in one hour while the second person requires three hours to learn the same material.

Thanks to women's Lib, now we not only have to be terrific moms and wonderful wives, but we have to be successful at our careers. What women's Lib gave us were choices, but was one of these staying home with our children? Did they realize that we might want to despite all the years of schooling we endured to have careers?

Men and women are not equal they are different.

Men lie and cheat.
Women change their mind.

It's a man's world because women love their daughters but are in love with their sons.

Many professional women are not interested in attaining the same level of success as a man. Once a woman has children and is still working outside the home, her emphasis changes.

We can't change the world by changing our daughters, but by changing our sons.

People get addicted to gambling because it is an erratic form of gratification. It has no pattern. It is like noise. There is no pattern. Music has a pattern.

If you never know when happiness, success or gratification will come, you are in limbo always waiting or trying. You can't stop this kind of behavior because there is no pattern. It can happen with a relationship. A person becomes addicted to another and can't get off from them. You must just stay away.

The difference between the person who won the gold and the person who won the silver; they wanted it more.

There is a time in everyone's life when they shine (i.e. for some it is kindergarten, for others it might be high school) for me it will be when I am forty.

I'm still not as old as I think I am.

Life is like sports. It is fun to play with people who play as well as you (sometimes you win and sometimes you don't). You don't get better if you play with people who play worse then you; you just look good. But if you play with people who play better than you; you get better and are constantly being challenged.

When you don't speak the same language, you miss a lot, namely jokes, riddles, sarcasm and innuendoes.

Conflict and resentment arise when people can't say what it is they want to say.

In families when conflict arises and members no longer speak, it is akin to a divorce. One person usually gets the family and all the invitations.

When does childhood end? When magical thinking escapes you and the summers no longer seem to last forever. When does adulthood begin? When you cannot only learn from your own mistakes but from others. In between you are discovering yourself.

When I was sixteen I worked in a children's shoe store. One of the salesmen was thirty-six at the time. When I was thirty-six I took my son to a children's shoe store and there was the same salesman now fifty-six. To me he looked exactly the same. Perhaps to a sixteen year old, thirty-six and fifty-six look no different.

My only wish is that I had invented Velcro.